Tidewater

Early and more recent poems

Gunnar Harding

Translated by
Robin Fulton and Anselm Hollo

MARICK PRESS

Library of Congress Cataloguing in Publication Data

Harding, Gunnar
Tidewater

ISBN 10: 1-934851-15-9
ISBN 13: 978-1-934851-15-9

Copyright © Gunnar Harding 2010
Copyright © Robin Fulton 2010
Copyright © Anselm Hollo 2010
Edited by Ilya Kaminsky
Design and typesetting by Sean Tai
Cover design by Sean Tai
Author photo by Gosia Stepien
Cover art by Józef Walczak, *Prometheus*, 2004, oil on canvas

Printed and bound in the United States

Marick Press
P.O. Box 36253
Grosse Pointe Farms
Michigan 48236
www.marickpress.com

Mariela Griffor, Publisher

Distributed by
Small Press Distribution
and
Wayne State University Press

Grateful acknowledgements to the publisher of ARS Interpres, Alexander Deriev, for his generous advice and support in bringing this book to fruition. This book was made possible to a collaboration between Ars Interpres and Marick Press.

CONTENTS

Tidewater   1

SELECTED POEMS 1967-1973

They Killed Sitting Bull   5
It's Evening When You Turn Back   6
Victoria Morland Where Are You Now   9
The Discoverers   13
Sweden   15
'What Do You Mean by This Poem'   16
Love in the Police Quarters   17
Viet Nam   19
O Marie Laveau   21
Buddy Bolden's Original Jass & Ragtime Band   22
Neon   25
January 1970   26
We All Saw Him   27
The New Washing-Machine   28
On the Way to Little Big Horn   29
Strange   30
Captain Blood   32
For Janet Persson   34
Adolescence   35
September Song   36

MORE RECENT POEMS

The Enchanted World of the Fairytale   41
Many Were Here, But They Left Again   42

TIDEWATER

Where the alphabet ends, the universe begins
with formlessness that casts the mind back
to the reader in which the sturdy cart-horse from the Ardennes
still trudges along on its big shoes.
All the words begin with capital letters
as if they were names of people we once knew
or places where we once were
and never returned to.
Next to each letter stands an animal.
Learn the letter, and the animal is yours.
You can build a cage for it out of a matchbox
with bars of sewing thread.
But the rat bites the boy who doesn't want to go to school.
The cart-horse kicks him.
The magpie steals his silver spoon, it is gone forever
but the coffee cups keep reappearing
with their glazed immortelles, slightly precious
gold-rimmed images of life as we'd like to think of it.
A cloud of steam rises out of every cup.
Above the water, more gigantic clouds rise
and become subjects for conversation, or perhaps even
conversations themselves, an exchange of thoughts still so formless
that they must be confronted with those of others
before they can acquire more precise outlines.
Everything comes in as flotsam, jetsam
carried by waves that have beaten against your shores for so long
they have become replicas of your thoughts:
pieces of broken coffee cups, magpie feathers, bits of conversation,
but all the silver that's left is these reflections on the water.
Only three letters remain, Y, E, and S.
They form the magical word.
Pronounce it, and the white suit is yours.

You win free admission to the shores of forgetfulness
where you can open up to the most elemental:
to look out across the sea, to think without words.

1990

Translated from the Swedish by Anselm Hollo

SELECTED POEMS 1967-1973

Translated from the Swedish by Robin Fulton

THEY KILLED SITTING BULL

they killed Sitting Bull. they
pressed his head down, on the ground
but it went on talking. they
pressed it harder on the ground
and it stopped talking. they
pressed his voice firmly in the ground
and under their feet the ground
began talking

IT'S EVENING WHEN YOU TURN BACK

the dead man is still hanging
in the diningroom chandelier. his black
patent-leather shoes nudge your hair when
you're eating dinner

the gendarmes have moved in. they're
   writing out
arrest warrants on the tablecloths which
   they tear
in strips and wind into the typewriters
you see everything clearly like someone
   returning
from a journey and seeing his apartment
   again
after a long absence

they have waited here for many years
played cards on the floorboards
and squirted sodawater at the bedbugs

the police officer moves a chess piece
'stranger when you pass by ...'

2

there is no time. everything is happening
now
within you. that summer
you think is long past is going on now
within you

you are five you are ten
you are twenty-eight and still sitting
leafing through a batch of old *Allers* from
    1916
when the aeroplanes were big summer
    butterflies
with red white and blue rings on their wings
and the American soldiers were little tin
    soldiers
with puttees and scout hats

you built a puppet theatre
with old cigar boxes

(the warm scent of old cigar boxes
and the bees outside the window)

3

the Indians are standing lined up on the
    horizon
wrapped in their blankets. they are waiting

the little scout soldiers have surrounded
    them
the little butterfly planes are whirring in
    the air

they drop fire from the sky
the Indians catch fire one by one

you look out of the window
the horizon is level again

4

there is no order except the order
you create yourself. everything is a mess
and is happening now and you can't raise
   the window
the farmworkers out there have blue overalls
and have strings in their hands. you pull
the strings and they rise high
over the green earth. you're hanging
on a string in the puppet theatre. a lonesome
   child
is talking above your head while the grass
   is dying
outside the window

with shut-off engines the aeroplanes vanish
   behind the sun

5

he drew his hand across the chessboard
sweeping all the pieces to the floor
'you don't understand this. you're not
up to the tactical game'

'cut the body down' he went on then
in his monotonous voice

VICTORIA MORLAND WHERE ARE YOU NOW

1
when this poem begins you've been
changed into a house. your eyes
are windows and far left
a woman. she wipes the glass so her image
can be seen and who walks by out there
but a young poet who looks just like you

the woman smiles in your eyes when she sees
him observing her with appreciation
this is the first day on earth. she
sees the sun for the first time. then comes
the snow and everything is as if stained
what is the young poet up to
this wonderful winter day when the ink
is frozen in the inkwell? he takes
his newly sharpened pencil and puts
out her eyes. he invents a
butterfly and lets it vanish across the snow
while he observes the world through the
partern
in the lace curtains

2

it is reality but at the same time
only an old film you don't understand
for all the time you want to turn it into
something else which you don't understand
either

you remember only fragments: he (Joseph Cotten)
comes back from the war to look up
Victoria Morland (Jennifer Jones)
was now ruins. it was
September. an old newspaper blew through
the streets. her picture on all the pages

you come back from the war
and look for Victoria Morland
who no longer exists

3

she no longer lives here in the white house
with the bicycle outside. no-one lives there
a thick layer of greasy dust dampens every
sound
the old man on the "Tomte" soap tin. Death
and love. you discovered them at the same
time. saw

the old man with a tin in his hand with
an old man with a tin in his hand with
an old man with a tin in his hand etc for ever
although the figures became too small to
be seen
by the naked eye. saw

the red specks on her dress
spread over the whole room. saw
the contours rubbed out. she. the white house.
you don't remember any more

4

was it her – the gold-tanned girl
on the beach? her body
was a face. you saw her body
which talked to you by the sea

you took up your blue notebook
and wrote: "your mouth is a boat
seen from below through running water,

her face rises towards you
out of the sand. a word is born
between her wet lips

you are lying on the beach
the waves are washing over you
and that's all you can see

5

he wipes his pencil on
his jacket sleeve. he sketches a train
that's setting off again. he sketches
bees and pollen blowing through
the carriages. men in blue laying
rails straight into the future. he sketches
a beginning as if nothing had happened
Victoria! she smiles. she is alive again

he runs towards her
but the distance only increases
he is running towards her

the house behind him emits
a silent chloroformed music
someone is hurrying through the empty rooms
banging all the doors shut behind her

THE DISCOVERERS

you don't remember where this journey
began. you remember only
a frontier control a city in ruins
the violet sparks from two cats
fighting in a bomb-shattered house

completely silent when the engine stopped
and yet you didn't hear that he
had come out to the car thrust
his hand in through the side window

in the shed with the scorching stove
sat a woman   stamped red stars
over everything

2

we are in the outskirts of America
we are in Asia or Africa
a desolate dry windless wasteland

the petrol station is trembling in the heat
a black dog is asleep on the warm concrete
the flies are buzzing round the petrol pump
it's a worn film from the thirties

they have come in through the door
but the pianola goes on
playing. we stand at the door
in long black coats. the black dog
has got up. you observe him

through your camera viewfinder shrunk
down to a beetle

the automatic pianola goes on playing

3

the dog has got up comes
out to the car. the window doesn't go up
you open the door it comes in. you look
   down
in the book again can't even read the
   chapter-headings
sit quiet in the front seat hear people
quietly growing up out of the ground

somewhere nearby
the whirr of a cine camera
photographing the flies

SWEDEN

      the statue of liberty
this statue is called. so huge
a grand piano can
    go into her nose. so beautiful
  only the drowning can see
her face
     and her torch lights up
  a new world
     above this one
        as in an El Greco picture
    where the light is stronger than here
     and all the people taller
      and more beautiful. it's so cold
     there
despite the fire
   and we're chilled in the wind
  that keeps rising
      and we move closer to each other.
     the earth
       has begun spinning more
      rapidly
     when we lower our voices we see
   four seasons pass
in an instant. it's autumn again
and the houses bob like lanterns in the
   storm. in each house
  sits a lonely person
     sits
    deep in his armchair
      and flies

'WHAT DO YOU MEAN BY THIS POEM'

      I would like
          to stride out of this poem
and kiss you on the mouth
            but I'm stuck. yet it feels
       natural
         as if
we were on our way somewhere

LOVE IN THE POLICE QUARTERS

      in the dark the bloodstains
        on the towels disappear
      in the dark
    his hands shape
her body. her
      hands his body
        he has leather boots
          & a huge baton
'if we put the light on
   we'd disappear'
      she whispers
  clings fast
  to the dark. we
    must say what
      everyone says
find the words
   which won't betray us. now
      everything is simpler

a car
passes outside the window
      the headlights
    wander over the walls
   illuminate the instruments of torture
  the portraits of the generals
  now she sees
     that he's dead. his face
    swaddled in white bandages

she begins gently winding off the bandages
   wincing against the strong
   interrogation light

and she says:
>'not only the victims
>must be identified
>but also the executioners'

she is standing in profile
  against the window
her eyes are filled
with tears

VIET NAM

    always it's just a thin wall
   separating us from them. they are
nearer us
    than the leaves and the rain here. you
   go through it
    from the beginning:
             'we are stuck together
    altogether. our hair
   mingles .. '
THE RAZOR BLADE
'our arms grow out
from the same body ...' through everything
   said
    is heard the knocking of a typewriter
        or machine-gun
           it increases. it
      disturbs me where I stand
     painting haloes on all the people
   in the bus queue.
         makes silence more real
       like death here. like
     the leaves here. they are
    burning
   already before they've fallen from
    the trees
only now the helicopter becomes
   visible up there against the blue. a body
    which is tossed out
        which tumbles
     writhes in the air. a face
    which sees
      the sky. the earth

                        but not you
        a face. it could not
            just as well
                    be yours

O MARIE LAVEAU

it's o.k. living in a
jungle but when it starts snowing
it gets too complicated. a parrot
with hoarfrost in its feathers flew heavily
ten years back. I went along
and came to New Orleans three weeks
after the death of George Lewis

o Burgundy Street you are my favourite
   street
Sweet Emma Barrett is sitting in her
   wheelchair
at the piano and everything's simple again
she has her vermilion handbag
on the piano-lid and small bells
on her slippers. o Marie Laveau
that voodoo queen way down yonder
in New Orleans

it's two weeks since the burial of George
Lewis. everyone dies and Sweet Emma
only gets uglier. thanks Kid Thomas
for Tishomingo Blues. we'll go home
in 4/4 time swinging our umbrellas
in the air

BUDDY BOLDEN'S ORIGINAL JASS & RAGTIME BAND

o all the people were gone about mad when
Buddy Bolden's band played in Lincoln Park
New Orleans in the summer of '93. and all
   the whores
in New Orleans went out of their wits when
   Buddy played
If You Don't Like My Potatoes Why do You
   Dig
So Deep and the young clarinettist with
the French Opera Alphonse Picou got so
   confused
he began to play the piccolo tune in
High Society on his clarinet and went on
playing it without a break for forty-eight
   hours

Buddy Bolden sat in his barber's shop
on Franklin Street and guffawed
as if to burst. he understood he'd
hit upon something quite new and he
called it *Jatz* or *Jass*. that was how
it began and it hasn't come to a finish yet

2

there's a lot we have Buddy Bolden
to thank for. he filled the streets
with music and warmth for fourteen years.
   there's
only one photo of him and it's
pretty blurred. in the photo you see

also two clarinettists. one with a large
drooping moustache and one lacking
a face. they're standing in front of
    something like
a tentcloth that gently stirs as if
a white horse were galloping behind it.
inside the tent it's snowing. it's cold
and the only warmth comes from a small
iron stove and Buddy Bolden's trumpet

3

he blew too hard. everyone said he was
blowing too hard. they said he's going
to blow the brains out of his skull. that was
what more or less happened

it was out in the sunshine during
the 1907 Big Parade in New Orleans
and Mahogany Hall shone whiter than
ever with the windows full of naked
girls and ostrich feathers. Buddy Bolden
led all the city's bands down Canal Street

when he put the trumpet to his lips
to blow his parade number Funky Butt
Funky Butt Take it Away suddenly it went
totally silent. there came not a sound from
the trumpet. the music was forced back
up in his head and rushed round in his
brain like an insane tramcar. he
carried on blowing until it looked
as if the trumpet would straighten out when
    all
of a sudden something inside him burst

all the people stopped and watched him
as he just fell down in the street
without a sound. not a sound was heard in
   the whole city
the ambulance came gliding slowly as in
   a dream
without sirens and the crowd parted
to let it through. they lifted up Buddy
   Bolden
and not even a click was heard
when the doors were shut behind him

4

all the mirrors were cracked as well in
the mental hospital. year after year. a long
crack right across his face. in blue-
striped pyjamas he paints a big placard
at his bedside

   Buddy Bolden's
   Original Jass
   & Ragtime Band

a tramcar he says electric and mad
in a light blue New Orleans at the bottom of
the sea. silence, not even white bubbles
to the surface. not even a surface. in '31
he found his trumpet put it to his lips
and cracked all the windows in the tramcar
with a single note. the water hurtled into it
was reason returning, then death
at 11 o'clock in the morning

NEON

        all the neon-signs are portraits
    of us. they surround us
take our lives
     and transform us into dead objects
    that change colour
        when the light changes colour.
       unclad
as dummies
     they lie on the bed
  her naked thighs
    glide over his. for a moment
they understand
    they are alive
        are hair and skin
    and bone and blood. for a moment
the nylon stocking
  falls gently
     to the floor. the smoke
    coils back
      into the chimney
        on the other side of the
        street.
  they switch the light off
but their thoughts
    run in neon letters
       across the house facades

JANUARY 1970

       what we need is
    the collapsible man
        who can be put into a briefcase
and be forgotten. like a miner
  they have downed tools
         but no-one notices it
the ways up
    are walled in. power
      exists here perpetually
   translated into
      typewritten stencils
   machine-guns
        picked apart. oiled
 in wooden boxes. people
picked apart bit by bit
        while waiting. you try to sort
     this out
  put it together
    but life runs out in the joints
continues under the ground. no voices
       can be heard
  but the knockings get stronger and
   stronger
     and tell us the situation is calm
      and despairing
        but the airconditioner
     is still working

WE ALL SAW HIM

eastwards there was someone who said we
can't travel eastwards and come to
San Francisco. it was the next day
that General Custer was elected president
and we fled from the cocktail parties
through fifteen states and it started raining
as it does in poems when something of
   consequence
has occurred

the whole car was full of people. there were
David and Daisy and Anselm and Hannes
and Arlene and Marybeth and Lotta and
Jan Sczcepanski. we had our pockets full
of potato crisps and ready mixed drinks
in little medicine bottles but there was no-one
exactly happy. we went on westwards
in the dawn and the rain went on and it was to
go on for four years

the newspaper where General Custer stood on his
white marble stair in his white marble city
crowning the year's Miss White Cherry Blossom
we stuffed in our boots to keep out
the damp. it was too late. everywhere
we saw dead Indians like large bloody
birds among the corn fields

when we set up camp on the river bank we saw him
Crazy Horse. it was in the night
west of the Mississippi. flowers were growing
out of his armpits. we saw his seed a white cloud
on its way through the Universe

THE NEW WASHING-MACHINE

we were so pleased at first when the new
washing-machine came. it was an exact
image of my head where wet underclothes
twirl round like poems in a perpetual
din. it is an exact image
of this house where my wife and daughter
cower in the middle of a huge centrifuge
while the waves clash above their heads

when they came to fetch the piano we
understood
we'd been cheated. we were playing it
even as they lifted it onto the lorry platform
soon they'll come to fetch us as well
and this house will stop breathing
the washing-machine will go on singing to itself

camerados. let's go. the water's streaming down
like Walt Whitman's beard. this country
isn't ours any more than this
washing-machine. our country lies far
from here. we are the blue-clad captains
on a white steamboat on our way to Mariefred
or Corsica

ON THE WAY TO LITTLE BIG HORN

when we came nearer we noticed
the long caravan of cars wasn't
moving. all the cars were abandoned wrecks
but the broken headlights were still shining
westwards. in the back seats
the children were sobbing hysterically.
    the young
woman who'd lost her husband blew her nose
and said she'd become so ugly

I became frightened when the dogs jumped up
on me. the large white naked albino
alsation had always made me suspicious
the policeman who bobbed up out of
    nothing had a
cowboy hat on his head or was it
Lord Baden-Powell who bobbed up in
    the snowstorm
with a pocket torch in his hand?

there was nothing to do. we wrote a letter
to the drugstore ordering two bottles
of red wine and a box of ammunition.
    'My husband
could have helped you' said the woman but it
wasn't true. however it was he was dead
    or with
his girl friend in St Louis. I laid my ear to
    the ground
and felt my head fill with the thunder from
thousands of horses on their way towards us

STRANGE

there's a soft billowing rhythm
   even in nightmares. when the
  students
 have been driven away in black cars
all the upstanding apes gather
   on a hill
  and bite each other
Nixon rises up. beneath the dark-curled wig
 his head is a lightbulb
  with the disadvantage
    that it has to be shaved
  twice a day. someone
    presses the button
 he shines
   breathes
 talks
    almost like a human
   being
the Swedish home minister applauds
 energetically
 'the ideologies limit our freedom'
  he says
    in astonishingly good
   English
 and both laugh
ho ho ho ho. thus everything is swamped
    in bird twittering
   and it's hard to hear
  what's said. over the dancers
a yellow cloud blossoms
   butterflies

>   grasshoppers
> or a shower of sparks. it's
>   impossible to distinguish

CAPTAIN BLOOD

for Che Guevara

it's Tuesday evening on TV and they're
showing Captain Blood. the ship approaches
off the coast he's standing on the bridge
observing the fortress through his telescope
it's impossible says the helmsman they have
over fifty cannon and we but eight. they have
five of our men captive there says Captain
   Blood
(we break off for a short commercial
the goddess of liberty emerges on the screen
   her hair
full of paper curlers. it's some new
detergent. she scrubs and scrubs
the stains won't budge. it's some old
stage-play)

a doctor what this country needs is
a doctor. the ship approaches glides
slowly past the sleeping marina
north of Miami. he's sitting on the first-aid chest
in the prow oiling a pistol. his clothes
are full of dead insects. he coughs quietly
and the wind fills the sails

*hello gringos. green grow
the bills* you sang as you marched
over the border with your pockets full of green
paper money. the sea is red. it's
sunrise. someone has put a burning
cigar far down in the corner of the star-

spangled banner
it's morning. the stars pale
one by one

FOR JANET PERSSON

    heute ist es strahlende Sonne
       und wolkenloser Himmel. German
      grammar
           is eternally invariable
              like old class-mates. we all
        once had a class-mate
    called Janet Persson
         who wrote letters
             to a woman's weekly
asking
   how to become an air-hostess. der Himmel
ist so blau
     so blau. we knew
        you'd never
           make it. so
        many who never make it. your
         hands were too big
   through the wall-bars
  in the gymnasium you are still looking
       towards the sky. high up there
    sways
      die Lufthansa. down here
you're slowly
    burning to ashes
in hopeless protest
      against loneliness

ADOLESCENCE

was it the Sports Palace in 1952? a whole
  school-class
     vanished in the green water
they don't surface again
       until today
     and I feel the strong odour
   of chlorine in my nostrils. we were
  shut in
       like all the dusty birds
      in the biology room. all the
     exits barred
by a white-dad catering woman
      who filled the whole world
       with her mighty bosom
     teachers
   and reserve officers. law
  and order. there was nothing else to do
but let the air out of assistant Furstenberg's
  bicycle
      and get lost
       on all the pathfinding
        exercises
year after year
     the boy in the tarzan-briefs
       has bounced up and down on
       the trampoline.
  with a shrill roar of his breaking voice
he dives into the water
     to look in the silence
      at the girls' legs. but they are all
     married now
    and rolled up in lilac-coloured
    bathrobes

SEPTEMBER SONG

I

september
     and all the women have moved south
  and only remain
naked and brown
       on the wall-almanacs in the transport
      cafe
in the gaily coloured bathing huts at the
  coast
     people drink tea with a lot of milk
          and watch
       the last sailing boats return
   trains
pass in all directions
     through tunnels of still green trees

at Aunt Gretta's summer-place Kvitterberga
    they're still playing croquet
  but everyone's sad
and goes around in white clothes
      just like Gustav V
       in a decisive tennis set. soon
    everything'll change and vanish
  like the little princesses
       and Fred Astaire

two croquet balls have rolled away. they
  are lying close together
    under an apple-tree. far from there
someone is seeing the earth
       as a little green ball

2

    will nothing of this
endure. someone lays aside
          Dagens Nyheter
      on a garden table
        and answers: no. under the tree
right beside the croquet balls
    lies an apple. almost rotten

our daughter
    walks between us. we have three heads
      and six feet
          we want to stay here
        with the yellow leaves
      twirling round our feet
    change
      into three trees
    but we must go on
there's so much here to see. the sun
  is streaming down
      and I don't know
    whether I'll laugh or cry
it's so long since I was a child
      and I've read
        too many books

3

    we catch the trains
travel
    northeast or southwest
      in red-brown carriages filled with leaves
everything is shaking. everything

              is rattling. the walls
  are of china
     and enclose us like egg-shell
        our heads
        move forwards through the world. words
    pass through our mouths
make everything visible. keep
           us warm
       LEAN OUT OF THE WINDOW
you're travelling forwards, travelling
   homewards. only those
      who stand still
    are moving backwards
outside the windows

MORE RECENT POEMS

Translated from the Swedish by Anselm Hollo

THE ENCHANTED WORLD OF THE FAIRYTALE

The smallest common denominator is a great sense of loss.
Dead deer dash past.
The green hunter loses sight of his quarry.
His quarry is what he loses sight of.
All he wants is to lose sight of his quarry.
The greatest common denominator is a leaf-green sense of loss.
Of three who went out, only one ever returned.
His success was complete, his reward boundless.
The eyeglasses of the less fortunate were never recovered.
They are washed by rain after rain.

They see ticks drop down on people
to inflame their brains with German landscapes.
Of three who went forth, there always were two who never returned.

Their defeat was complete, their loss boundless.
There are days when the giant won't fall for the ruse,
days when no kindly mammals speak to us
with human voices.
Dead deer dash past.
The forest comes alive with whispers: Can we go now?
But no trail leads out of a leaf-green sense of loss.
Dopey, the vulnerable dwarf
scrapes his stepmother's fiddle,
kisses a coffin of glass.

MANY WERE HERE, BUT THEY LEFT AGAIN

1

Many were here, but they left again.
Only a few extras
still stand around, forlorn, in the parking lot.
Perhaps they never existed, yet I know
they'll come back one day, just as November
always comes back. We know the season
and into our nostrils rises a cold smell of iron
heralding its arrival

glassy afternoons in vibrating apartments
with mirrors mounted on doors, reflecting themselves
and other mirrors beyond them, painted white.
A stationary storm. I walk around in there
and the air doesn't hurt me,
doesn't move me, it touches but doesn't move me.
I stand in there and vibrate,
supplicating, stationary, mirrored.

Not a prayer but a wound,
not a wound but a prayer
that yesterday's clowns will return
for a Special Additional Performance
so one can find out if their suffering is so heart-rending
that it once again causes tears to spatter on the panes
and laughter to move
in piles of dry leaves rife with polio.

So much brick.
I have to smile.
So much brick
to show what we feel, deep down.

2

Then comes this gray light from the future
and it is terrifying.
The underground carnival continues, a masque
of worms with papier-mâché faces.
Their smiles are only a row of teeth.
Rotting seed pods. They live in them.
Hear their rattles
across the ground under the trees
slowly pulling their darkness over themselves.

Then the procession gathers, detaches itself
and stumps through sleet, tracks and foretells in the snow,
in coffee grounds, a future in black and white, with the black
slowly devouring the white until Spring comes, or death,
with birdsong in the all-white cherry-trees.
Will we be surprised once again
on the outskirts of some divine comedy
where, in awkward bliss and bashful ecstasy,
even the wingless soar
on balmy winds in too diaphanous garments?
Will, in a dance, everything fill with grace,
feet stride on pavements
reborn into a renaissance
in which blood rushes through marble veins?

All want out and into the light. Look at me!
So many! But all we can see is the teeming crowd.
Here they foregather who will become piles of dead leaves
drifting across a cold gray afternoon. A prayer,
the teeming of dry leaves.
Suddenly, they fly up to their branches again
and the trees take a bow.
The prompter goes on whispering unused lines.

But it's all over, everybody has gone home,
everybody but one.
He sees the brown leaves rise.
He thinks he is dreaming.
He is dreaming.

3

We've forgotten the clowns, it all started with them;
but over time, purity of heart has become less significant.
They hide in the crowd. They are safe there.
Hardly anyone knows what they look like
when their *tristesse* no longer smiles
its nose-bleed-colored smile.
When tears have washed away all the greasepaint
there remains only an embittered schoolteacher
convulsively clutching the edge of a desk
in a dead man's grip.
It was all a dream about feelings, amplified
to a cock's crow in some broken language.
Who is still interested in climbing, rung by rung,
up to a moon made of glass?
And yet the procession moves on
in the night that lets us see all.

They walk their sleep, walk it back here,
the sound of tin whistles fills rooms, walk dawns
to slake the lime, switch off the lamps.
The small jar contains the daylight,
the large one all the tears wept on their graves.
No wind but the ashes of an ocean.
The question is not where to but past and the answers:
to recognize this ocean in small puddles

and to let it billow in "no wind,"
to chase off the dog that is chewing its own bone
and to wake the sleepwalker
on the ever-receding shore of waves of rooftiles.

BOOKS BY MARICK PRESS

The Dropped Hand by Terry Blackhawk. ISBN 978-0-9779703-3-9
Never Night by Derick Burleson. ISBN 0-9779703-5-3
Emily Ate the Wind by Peter Conners. ISBN 978-0-9712676-4-0
  (Hardcover); ISBN 978-0-9779703-9-1 (Paperback)
The Blue City by Sean Thomas Dougherty. ISBN: 0-9779703-5-3
American Prophet by Robert Fanning. ISBN-13 978-1-934851-01-2
The Seed Thieves by Robert Fanning. ISBN 0-9779703-0-2
Storm by Katie Ford. ISBN 978-0-9712676-8-8
White Holes by James Hart III. ISBN 0-9779703-1-0
Folding A River by Kawita Kandpal. ISBN-13 978-0-9712676-3-4
The Fortunate Islands by Susan Kelly-DeWitt. ISBN 978-0-9712676-6-4
Been and Gone by Julian Kornhauser. Translated by Piotr Florczyk.
  ISBN-13 978-1-934851-05-0
The Boy Who Killed Caterpillars by Joshua Kornreich.
  ISBN 978-0-9712676-7-1
A Complex Bravery by Robert Lipton. ISBN 0-9712676-1-8
It Might Do Well with Strawberries by David Matlin.
  ISBN-13 978-1-934851-02-9
The Sleeping by Caroline Maun. ISBN 0-9712676-2-6
At the Revelation Restaurant and Other Poems by Alicia Ostriker.
  ISBN-13 978-1-934851-06-7
Solute by Daniel Padilla. ISBN 0-9779703-2-9
The Country of Loneliness by Dawn Paul
As When, In Season by Jim Schley. ISBN 978-1-934851-00-5
Witness of Music by Alexander Suczek. ISBN 0-9779703-8-8
Father, Tell Me I Have Not Aged by Russell Thorburn.
  ISBN 0-9779703-6-1
Homage to Paul Celan by G.C.Waldrep. ISBN 0-9779703-4-5
The Catfish by Franz Wright. ISBN-13 978-0-9712676-9-5
INRI by Raul Zurita. Translated by William Rowe.
  ISBN-13 978-1-934851-04-3
Leave Me Hidden by Pulitzer Prize winner Franz Wright.
  ISBN-13: 978-1-934851-10-4
The Country of Loneliness by Dawn Paul. ISBN-13 978-1-934851-07-4
Wish List by Gerry LaFemina. ISBN-13 978-1-934851-09-8
Escape by Mary Sanders Smith. ISBN-13 978-1-934851-11-1

www.ingramcontent.com/pod-product-compliance
Lightning Source LLC
LaVergne TN
LVHW011431080426
835512LV00005B/377